Make It Happen: The no-nonsense guide to publishing and marketing your ebook

Louisa Dang and Lisa Logan

Copyright © 2018 Louisa Dang, Lisa Logan

All rights reserved.

ISBN: 1717008569
ISBN-13: 978-1717008565

Disclaimer
The goal of this book is to serve as an easy reference guide for writers who would like to become independent authors, selling ebooks on Amazon and other platforms. It is not intended to be a comprehensive guide to self publishing or a replacement for legal or other expert advice. While we have made every effort to ensure that all information in this book is accurate and up-to-date, inaccuracies may exist. We accept no liability or responsibility for any loss or damage inadvertently caused by following the advice in this book.

ABOUT THE AUTHORS

Louisa Dang is a freelance writer and editor. She earned her M.F.A. in creative writing at North Carolina State University, and her short stories and articles have appeared in publications throughout North Carolina, including *Alamance Magazine*, *Bishop House Review*, *Our State*, *Triad Living*, and the *North Carolina Literary Review*. She is the editor of *JUMP! The magazine for creative kids!* (www.jumpforkids.wordpress.com) and blogs at www.southernbendbooks.com. You can check out her books at https://www.smashwords.com/profile/view/LouisaDang

Lisa Logan is a screenwriter, novelist, and journalist from North Carolina. Her novel *House of Mirrors* is available on Amazon at http://ow.ly/k2vC0. Lisa Logan started out writing articles for *Our State* magazine and profile articles for the *N.C. Literary Review*, interviewing various North Carolina authors of fiction. Her own creative works were published in several issues of the Raleigh *News and Observer*'s short fiction section "Sunday Reader." Lisa's passion for screenwriting led to freelancing for a national screenwriter's magazine *Creative Screenwriting* in which she wrote features, interviewing Hollywood screenwriters, high-level film producers, directors, and actors.

CONTENTS

1 HOW TO USE THIS GUIDE

Ready to become an independent author? This guide gives you all the tools you need to successfully publish and promote your ebook! We've combined our own experience as self-published authors with information we've gathered from loads of references to give you only the most pertinent information you need to get started.

Although our primary focus is publishing via Amazon, many of these tips can also be used to help sell your books using other platforms. Use this book as a reference tool, picking and choosing the parts you need, or read it straight through. We've organized the guide into easy-to-use sections, in the rough order that you'll need to publish and promote your book:

• Setting the stage for publication – book covers, ISBN, front and back matter...

• Formatting your manuscript for publication

• Publishing to Amazon's Kindle Direct Publishing program

• Pre-launch logistics!

• Launching your book with power selling tips!

• FAQs and press release help

2 INTRODUCTION

Welcome to our newest guide to publishing and marketing your ebooks! When we published our first guide in 2013, indie publishing was a relatively new concept that many writers had just started to explore. Today, the dust has settled, and more and more writers have published their own ebooks (and print books!).

With high-quality indie books being published every day, the stigma once attached to self-publishing has faded, and indie books are receiving awards and being sold in bookstores across the world! Indie publishing is now seen as a viable option for writers who want full creative control over their work, from what appears on the cover, to how they market their books.

Our last guide focused on Amazon's KDP Select as being one of the best ways to publish and promote your ebooks. KDP Select has helped independent authors increase their books' exposure and helped Amazon to dominate the ebook industry by requiring authors to digitally publish their books exclusively on Kindle Select (https://kdp.amazon.com/self-publishing/KDPSelect).

While Amazon is still a huge player in the marketplace, writers now have many more options – in both ebook and print formats – for publication and marketing their own work. We'll discuss other major publishing platforms, such as Smashwords and Barnes & Noble, along with the pros and cons, to help you make the best decision for your book.

Authors today also have much more marketing know-how and tools than they did in 2013. From social media to online ads, writers can assert control over their platform. Blogging has been streamlined, we know more about Internet marketing trends, and we have improved analytics software to help target the ideal audiences for our books.

With all the available, inexpensive tools at our fingertips, indie writers have more options than ever! So, let's go and explore them!

3 GETTING READY FOR PUBLISHING

You've done the hardest part – writing and revising your manuscript! Now, it's time to get down to business and start the process of publishing your ebook. You'll need a last-minute check for mistakes, a cover, an author's bio, a blog or website, and ... Well, let's just get started!

Important!
In the next chapter, you'll learn how to format your manuscript for epublishing. Part of that will involve getting rid of all the styles in your document – so DO NOT spend hours nicely centering headings and adding fancy typesetting to your manuscript. Unlike print publishing, epublishing requires very little formatting. However, editing for content is obviously still important!

Editing on the Cheap

You may have had your beta readers, best friend, your mom, and your co-workers read your manuscript for clarity and general ideas, but they can't catch everything. If you can't afford to hire a professional editor, try one of the many free and inexpensive software editing tools.

The majority of these tools identify problems in your document like spelling errors, clichés, repeated words, overused filler words, too many adverbs, and grammatical mistakes. They highlight key phrases and words that need revising and generate separate "reports" or sidebars with more detailed information.

Carla King, a writer for BookBaby Blog, has put together a great list of nine manuscript editing programs at **http://blog.bookbaby.com/2017/10/nine-manuscript-editing-software-programs-reviewed/**.

Most programs range from as little as $10 per month or $30 per year to $140 per year. Some offer "lifetime memberships" for a very reasonable price. ProWritingAid (**https://prowritingaid.com/en/App/Purchase**), a tried-and-tested tool that has been around for years, offers a lifetime membership for $175!

While such tools are a great help for pointing out blatant errors (and alerting the author to their own bad habits!), remember that they use algorithms – not human editors – to analyze your manuscript. Software tools aren't great at picking up on nuanced issues like tone, pacing, and character development.

Hiring a Professional Editor

If you can afford to hire a professional editor, be sure to do your homework first. Not all editors are the same! They should ask you to send them a few pages of your manuscript, so they can see what kind of writing you do and how much work it needs.

Then they can give you a more accurate estimate of how much they'll charge. If your editor lives in another country, be sure they have experience with the language and dialect of your book.

Proofreaders

Proofreading is NOT the same as copy editing – proofreaders check documents in their final stages for things like spelling, grammar, and punctuation errors. A proofreader will also check for typos and point out major layout or formatting mistakes, but he/she won't drastically alter the text or make any stylistic changes to improve the flow of the document or how well it reads. You'll need a copy editor for those types of revisions.

A good proofreader should also catch any copyright problems, such as if you quote lyrics from a song without attributing them to the artist. They should point out inconsistencies, such as if you spell a character's name three different ways!

Copy editors

If you don't feel very confident in your grammar skills, you might want to invest in a copy editor. They will cost a little more than a proofreader because they look at your writing in more depth. As well as looking at grammatical issues, copy editors also check facts, legal and copyright issues, and writing style. They will point out if a sentence sounds "clunky," or if you already used the word "positive" three times in the same page!

Developmental editing

The most expensive and in-depth type of editing is developmental editing. These types of editors look at the "big picture." They look at plot, character development, structure, consistency of style, whether the tone is right for the audience, sentence structure … and more.

Resources

Editor Susan Buchanan of Perfect Prose (**https://perfectproseservices.com**/) gives a good overview of all the different types of editing on her website. She is also an excellent proofreader (Louisa has hired her before!).

The Editorial Freelancers Association (**https://www.the-efa.org/rates**/) lists the industry standard's prices for editing jobs. It also gives a guideline for how long each page should take to edit per hour.

Winning Book Covers

Judging a book by its cover is a reality in marketing ebooks and self-published print books. Think about it... When you enter a bookstore and you see a homemade-looking cover, you probably assume the writing is as bad as the cover. Call us shallow, but we do it, and so do thousands of shoppers out there. Purchasing decent-looking cover art is a necessity in selling your ebook.

When it comes to creating your ebook cover, you have lots of choices – you can do it yourself, hire a cover artist, or use the "cover creator" tool often included within book publishing software. As independent authors, we have used all three methods.

DIY covers

For her collection of short stories, *Up Pops the Devil*, Louisa tried to make her own "no-budget" cover from scratch, using Microsoft Word and free stuff. First, she used a free image of a car from Microsoft Office. Then she added text using Gimp free software (**http://www.gimp.org**/) downloaded onto her computer.

The result was breathtakingly bad:

For other DIY efforts, Louisa paid for royalty-free images and used her own photography to create more covers in Microsoft Word. These worked slightly better. But, unless you have some great cover art and a lot of patience, M.S. Word is not the best tool to create covers.

Today, we have **canva.com**. With canva, you can use free cover templates to create a professional-looking ebook cover. You can add your own pictures (or pay a little extra for royalty-free art) and text, then download the finished product.

This article by Jacqueline Thomas (https://www.canva.com/learn/book-cover-design-50-amazing-covers-you-will-want-to-pick-up/) gives some great tips on designing your ebook cover.

Hiring someone

Investing in someone who specializes in book cover design will cost you money, but you get what you pay for! Your designer will create a unique cover especially for your genre. Some designers specialize in romance, horror, fantasy, and just about any genre. So, do your research to find out who best fits your style.

The website The Creative Penn (https://www.thecreativepenn.com/bookcoverdesign/) has a huge list of individual book designers and designing companies you can browse.

Another option for finding a book cover artist is 99designs (**http://99designs.com**). On this site, you set up a contest for designers to submit their artwork for your book cover. You post the specifications, and they deliver their designs to you in the hopes of winning the award you post of at least $199.

Pre-made covers

An excellent option if you can't afford to spend a lot on a cover but need something a little more polished than the DIY-route is to buy a pre-made cover. There are hundreds of sites offering pre-made covers – all you do is have them insert your title and name. You pay a flat fee, and it's an easy way to get a great-looking cover. Lisa and Louisa have both had great luck with Go On Write (**https://www.goonwrite.com**) for their books.

Cover creation tools and help

If you are publishing with Amazon's KDP, you may want to use the Cover Creator feature. You provide the image, or you can select one from the gallery of stock images, and then you edit it. It's free, but the drawback is that you can only use the cover for KDP, not for other book publishing platforms.

Many publishers will design a cover for you for an additional fee. Barns and Noble press works with 99designs (mentioned earlier) to create a unique cover for your book.

Getting ideas

Before you make a final decision, browse the covers of the best sellers on Amazon's Kindle Store, especially the best sellers in your genre. Notice that some of the best book covers look good as thumbnails. Their titles are bold and readably sized. That's important to your mobile readers searching for a new book.

Another good rule of thumb is that shorter titles and big imagery seem to be a common factor in many successful books online. Does your title exude a feel for the genre? In other words, does it communicate that it's a romance novel or horror novel? Most importantly, make sure it looks professional. It may be worth $30 or more to buy a decent cover.

Do I Need an ISBN to Publish?

Contrary to popular belief, you don't need to spend hundreds of dollars to buy an ISBN in order to publish your book on Amazon. In fact, for KDP, you don't need an ISBN at all! Once your ebook is published, Amazon will assign it a 10-digit Amazon Standard Identification Number (ASIN), which will be unique to your ebook. If you decide to print your ebook, Amazon will assign you a different ASIN.

If you choose to publish your book entirely on your own or want to set up your own publishing company, you will need to purchase an ISBN. What is it exactly?

International Standard Book Number (ISBN) is a 10-digit number (for books published before 2007) or 13-digit number (for those published after January 1, 2007) used to identify one particular edition of a book. If your goal is to sell your book through different retail channels (like bookstores, libraries, universities, websites, etc...), you'll need an ISBN for each edition or title of your book to help those retailers order copies of and keep track of your book.

Each country has its own agency that assigns ISBNs. The agency that assigns ISBNs in the United States is commercial library services agency Bowker. You can buy an individual ISBN from the company's website (**https://www.isbn.org/**). But prices are high at $125 per ISBN, unless you're planning on buying in bulk.

Or you can let an online publisher like Smashwords pay for your ISBN. Because they publish thousands of titles a year, they pay bulk rates for ISBNs (1,000 ISBNs cost $1,000, so that's only $1 per ISBN). It works out great for them, and for you!

Front and Back Matter

Before you publish, it's important to decide on your "front" and "back matter." The pages before the body of the text – such as the cover, title page, and contents – are known as the "front matter." And, conversely, the pages at the end of your book are known as the "back matter." Both are important, as they're the first and last things readers see when viewing your book.

Since many publishers, including Amazon, offer free samples of the first few pages of books (letting customers see if they like the writing style, etc.), we can take advantage of this feature by having our books start as quickly as possible to pull readers in!

For example, in traditional print publishing, the order is typically as follows:

- cover
- title page
- copyright information
- dedication
- contents
- preface
- about the author (sometimes at the end in novels)
- introduction
- chapter 1 (body of book begins)
- last chapter (body of book ends)
- additional resources/appendices
- index
- credits

Nonfiction books might also include a list of figures and/or tables, and an established author will want to include a list of previously published works. This is a lot to include in an ebook, where readers expect to dive right into the story!

So, here's a closer look at what you might include in your ebook:

- **title page** – Optional, as you already have the title and byline on the cover. But you can use it to your advantage, including abbreviated copyright information on the same page.

- **copyright** – Personally, I like a reminder up-front that the work belongs to me! But other writers choose to move this information to the back of the book. As mentioned earlier, you could put an abbreviated copyright notice at the front and a more detailed one at the back.

- **dedication** – This is up to you. If you're dedicating your book to someone special, it might be a nice gesture to mention this up front, and as a reader, I always enjoy seeing heartfelt dedications ("To my mother, who inspired me to write this book..."). Otherwise, move this to the back.

- **contents** – If you're writing a novel, you probably don't need a table of contents for numbered chapters. If you're writing a nonfiction book, or a book with specific, unique chapters (such as a collection of short stories), definitely include a table of contents up front, so readers can easily navigate your book.

- **about the author** – If your background and expertise is key to the book you've written, put your author's bio up front. For example, you've written a how-to book on kayaking, and you've taught kayaking for the past 15 years – definitely mention this up front to add to your credibility. For novels, I would put bios at the back, along with your contact information.

- **additional resources/acknowledgements** – Keep these in the back, where readers can refer to them for more information if they need to.

- **samples of other works** – It is a great idea to include an excerpt from your other published works, or a teaser of an upcoming book. But with limited sample space, put this information in the back of the book.
- **blurbs** – "Blurbs" are positive quotes about your book from other authors. If you are lucky enough to have a blurb from a famous author in your genre, by all means include it up front (give it its own page!). But if your only blurbs are from your best friends (who aren't famous), keep them in the back! It's extremely frustrating having to scroll through pages of quotes from authors I've never heard of to get to the meat of the book!

Bottom line?

Use your best judgment, based on your specific type of book. Remember that you only have a few sample pages to capture readers' attention, so think about what is most important to include up front.

4 PICKING A PUBLISHER AND PREPPING

You're ready to publish your manuscript online. Now what? First, you'll need to pick a publishing platform, and then you'll need to follow their guidelines to format your manuscript. Don't worry – it's pretty straightforward! (Don't forget that you can always publish through more than one platform, unless you choose KDP Select.)

There are many different platforms that publish ebooks, and we will be focusing on publishing via KDP, but all the platforms follow the same basic pattern:

1. Save your manuscript as a Microsoft Word document
2. Format document and then save it as an HTML file
3. Preview ebook
4. Upload document to publishing site.

Who to Choose?

Before you dive in to Amazon KDP, you might want to explore other options, just to make sure you're getting the deal you want. Here's a quick overview of the top free platforms and their features:

Amazon KDP and KDP Select – royalties between 30% and 70% depending on list price of your book

Barnes & Noble Press – royalties between 40% and 65% depending on list price

Ibooks – royalties 70%

Draft2Digital – they take 10% off the retail price of each sale

Kobo – royalties between 45% and 70% depending on list price

Smashwords – royalties between 60% and 85% depending on whether you sell your book through another retailer or directly from the Smashwords site.

Amazon KDP and KDP Select

For the widest distribution of your book, Amazon's KDP is the best bet. You'll just need to decide if you want to do KDP or KDP Select. Amazon books can be read on Kindle devices and on any device with the free Kindle app, and authors have access to Author Central, which we talk about later in the book.

When you publish your book using KDP Select, you agree to make the digital format of that book available exclusively through KDP for at least 90 days. During those 90 days, you are not allowed to distribute your book digitally anywhere else, including on your website, blogs, etc. But you can still distribute your book in physical format, as a paperback or hardback.

At first, the program may sound kind of limiting – some writers like to publish their books on as many platforms as possible, including Smashwords and Barnes & Noble. But the upside to KDP Select is that you have the option to make your book available for free for up to five days every 90 days. This can be a great tool to increase your exposure as a writer.

And by using KDP Select, your book is eligible to be included in the Kindle Owners' Lending Library, which means that you earn royalties based on how frequently the book is borrowed. In addition, by choosing KDP Select, you will have access to other promotional tools, including Kindle Countdown Deals.

Barnes & Noble Press

(**https://press.barnesandnoble.com**/) B&N Press will publish your ebooks and sell them at bn.com, the nook, and any devices with the free nook app. The royalties are pretty straightforward, based on the list price of your ebook:
- For books priced $0.99 - $2.98, you get 40%
- For books priced $2.99 - $199.99, you get 65%

Barnes & Noble Press doesn't have as many bells and whistles as KDP. There is no equivalent to Author Central, and there are definitely less web pages devoted to helping self publishers.

iBooks

The only way to publish an ebook directly to Apple's iBooks is on a Mac. If you own a PC, you'll need to use what is known as an "aggregator," which is basically another business who will take your ebook and get it into Apple's iBookstore.

The only catch? Aggregators usually charge – some take

10% off the list price for each purchase. Others charge by page. Smashwords.com is an aggregator but takes 40% off your list price for sales to iBooks.

If you own a Mac, no problem! You can use iBooks Author to create your ebook and sell it in iBooks or in different formats. With Apple, you keep 70% of royalties.

Draft2Digital

(https://www.draft2digital.com/) D2D is the whole package – they will format your manuscript for epublishing, publish it, and distribute it to their digital bookstore partners, which include Amazon and iBooks. They don't charge for these services, but they do take 10% off the retail price of each book sale (which is 15% of net royalties).

It still sounds like a pretty good deal! And the reviews are good – authors say Draft2Digital is easy to use and efficient.

Kobo Writing Life

(https://www.kobo.com/us/en/p/writinglife) KWL will publish your book and add it to the Kobo catalogue, where readers can download ebooks to their Kobo device or to another device with the free Kobo app. Kobo also distributes your book to many online retailers, such as W.H. Smith in the United Kingdom. Reviews are generally positive, with most writers saying KWL is easy to use and to track sales.

But writers' opinions differ on whether or not they've sold more books using KWL as compared to other platforms. As with every project, the results usually depend upon how much effort you put into it!

Smashwords

(https://www.smashwords.com/) We have experience using Smashwords and find it to be a fairly easy process, and their site offers lots of support for authors. Smashwords will distribute your book in several different formats, including for Kindle, and will make it accessible to many online libraries and bookstores, including B&N, Kobo, and iBooks. But not Amazon as yet, unless you have made more than $2000 at Smashwords retailers.

If another retailer sells your book, you receive 60% - 70% of the list price. If you sell your book directly from the Smashwords website, you'll get 85% of the net proceeds (sales price minus PayPal payment processing fees).

Smashwords also lets you set up "coupons" so you can sell your book at a reduced price for a set amount of time. (Personally, I didn't have any luck with coupons and would rather just set my price lower for a time!)

Prepping Using Microsoft Word

You might be wondering which format to choose when uploading your manuscript to Amazon's KDP or another platform. For ease of use, the best choice is to start with Microsoft Word (.doc/.docx) and later save your document as an HTML file before publishing (we will explain how to do this later in the chapter).

However, KDP also accepts these formats:
- HTM, ZIP
- ePub (EPUB)
- Plain Text (TXT) – KDP does not support the use of images with plain text file
- Rich Text Format (RTF)
- Adobe Portable Document Format (PDF)

If you try to upload your manuscript as a PDF, you may run into conversion problems such as:
- irregularly bolded text
- irregular page breaks
- irregular font sizes
- inconsistent text flow
- missing or oversized images

So, for ease of conversion, your best bet is to format your manuscript in Microsoft Word!

Formatting Your Manuscript for Conversion

If you haven't done so already, save your entire manuscript as one MS Word document. Do not include the cover, as KDP will automatically embed the cover image later in the process. (If you are using another publishing platform, be sure to check how they want you to handle the cover-creation process.)

Go ahead and insert front and back matter, but don't worry about formatting them just yet. Next, you'll need to prepare your document to be converted into an ebook using the following guidelines. These steps will ensure that your book will be properly formatted when it's published as an ebook.

1. Remove all custom formatting by pressing CTRL+A to select the entire document, then clicking on "Normal" style from the "Home" tab.

Note: Your text will convert to the default settings (for example, Calibri 11), so if you don't like that font, you'll have to change it back. Kindle and other e-reader devices support a variety of typefaces, but it is best to avoid exotic ones, as there is no guarantee they'll be supported by all e-readers.

2. Delete page numbers, headers, footers, blank pages, and wingdings.

3. Go back through your document and reformat as needed:

- Center your title page and copyright information (and any other text you think should be centered) and bold them.
- Select Heading 1 style from the "Home" tab for the title to make it stand out.
- Replace any bold and italic text, bullets, and numbered lists.
- Select Heading 1 style for each chapter heading.
- For headings inside your chapters, click on Heading 2. For subheadings, click on Heading 3.
- Insert page breaks at the end of every chapter and every major section of your book where it makes sense to break up the text. (Select the "Insert" tab and then click on "Page Break.")
- Take out all extra spaces and empty lines of text where you don't need extra spaces – these will show up as large gaps in the Kindle book version. (To see all the spaces in your document more clearly, click on the "¶" symbol on the "Home" tab. Each space will now be represented with a dot, and each "Return" represented by the "¶" symbol.)
- Remove all tabs by using the "Find and Replace" function. For the "Find what" line enter ^t (the "caret t" is the symbol for tab) and then in the "Replace with" space don't enter anything. Then select "Replace All."
- Replace tabs with first-line paragraph indents not exceeding 1.5 inches. (On the "Home" tab, find "Paragraph" and then click the arrow in the bottom right hand corner. The "Paragraph" box will appear. Click "Special" and select "First Line" from the drop-down menu. Enter the desired indent measurement. See "Using Auto-indent" section for more details)

- To insert a graphic, select "Insert" and then "Picture." Use Center alignment. Do not copy and paste graphics. Resist the urge to resize your image – KDP will automatically size it for you. (If your book contains graphics, see "Books with Graphics" section later in this chapter.)
- KDP supports the use of tables. To insert a table, select "Insert" and then "Table."
- If you want to include hyperlinks, it's best to type in the entire web address, including the http:// or the link will not work. For some reason, Word's "insert hyperlink" feature is hit-or-miss and often does not work! For extremely long links, you can use a free service like bitly.com to shorten them.
- Remove all hyphens placed in the middle of words for line breaks. Line breaks won't look the same on ebook readers.

4. Insert a Table of Contents (see "How To create a Table of Contents" section later in this chapter).
5. Select "Save As" and save the document as a "Web Page, Filtered" (for PC) or "Web Page" (for Mac). This creates the HTML file that you will use when you publish your ebook to KDP.

Using Auto-indent for Microsoft Word

Once you remove all the tabs in your document, you'll need to insert first-line paragraph indents. Here's a basic guide for how to do that.

1. Press CTRL+A to select the entire document.
2. On the "Home" tab, click the little box with arrow on the "Paragraph" bar. The paragraph pop-up box appears.
3. Select the "Indents and Spacing" tab.
4. In the "Indentation" section, under "Special," click on the drop-down menu and select "First Line."

5.   In the "By" text box, press the up or down arrows to enter a number between 0.2 and 1.5 inches. Do not increase the number to more than 1.5 inches, or your indents will appear huge in Kindle! I use 0.2 inches.
6.   Click "OK."

How to Create a Table of Contents

A neatly structured and functional table of contents (TOC) provides easy navigation and a more pleasurable reading experience on an e-reader. Below are steps you can take to create an active table of contents for your ebook. Creating your TOC manually in Word gives you control over which sections you want to highlight in your TOC.

NOTE: KDP now has Kindle Create, which is free software you download onto your computer to help format your manuscript for publishing. Kindle Create pulls from your chapter headings to automatically create a TOC. This is helpful for novels but for non-fiction books you might want to also identify sub-sections, etc…

NOTE: Avoid using the TOC generator in Word because it inserts styles which can cause conversion problems for Kindle.

1.   If you haven't already done so, insert a page break after the last line of each chapter.
2.   After typing the title page and any front matter you wish to include, insert a page break where you would like to start the TOC.
3.   Now type "Table of Contents" at the top of the page and select Heading 1 style from the "Home" tab.
4.   Type out the chapter names in your book beneath "Table of Contents."
5.   Go to the first page of the first chapter and highlight that chapter name. (For instance,

highlight "Chapter One.")

6. In order to make the chapter name active, you will need to bookmark the destination that you want the TOC entry to take the reader to. After you have highlighted the chapter title, go to the "Insert" tab. In the "Links" section, select the "Bookmark" icon.

7. A bookmark screen will appear prompting you to enter the bookmark's name. Enter the name of your chapter. If there are spaces between the words, insert underscores instead because you can't use spaces or punctuation in bookmark names.

8. Click the "Add" button.

9. Go back to your Table of Contents page and highlight the chapter name again. (For example, highlight "Chapter One.")

10. Click on the "Insert" tab, and in the "Links" section, select the Hyperlink icon. Here, you are creating a hyperlink between the chapter name you highlighted in the TOC and the one you bookmarked earlier.

11. The "Insert Hyperlink" screen appears. In the "Link To" menu, click the "Place in This Document" button in the center because you're linking items within the document itself.

12. Now you will see a list of bookmarks in your document. For this example, you should see your first chapter name ("Chapter One"). Select it and click "OK." Now you'll see "Chapter One" as a hyperlink on the Table of Contents page.

13. Repeat steps 5-12 for each chapter in your book and for each section you would like to appear in the TOC.

Books with Graphics

If your book contains images, you'll need to perform an extra step before you can publish it to KDP, otherwise your images won't show up on Kindle readers. Don't worry – it's easy!

After formatting your document for KDP and saving it as an HTML file (a filtered web page), you'll notice an extra folder. This is because when you insert images into your ebook, your computer automatically creates this folder and places your graphic(s) in it.

For example, after I save my ebook, "MurderMystery," as an HTML file, a new folder appears named "MurderMystery_Files." Inside this folder are the graphics I inserted when creating my murder mystery ebook. Here's what to do next:

1. Right click on your HTML file (your ebook) and select "Send to" from the menu.
2. Click on "Compressed (zipped) folder."
3. A new folder will appear with the same name as your HTML file (for example, "MurderMystery") but it will have a zipper on it.
4. Drag the folder with your images ("MurderMystery_Files") into the new zipped folder. This basically groups your HTML document and your images together to be used when you publish your book to KDP.
5. When you publish your ebook to KDP, you will upload the zip folder instead of the HTML file.

Using Kindle Previewer

Kindle Previewer is a free tool that emulates how your book will look on Kindle devices and applications and shows how the text displays for any orientation or font size.

Once you've finished formatting your MS Word manuscript for KDP and saved it as a filtered web page, you can use Kindle Previewer to check the layout of your book and make sure it's displayed properly. You can also check that the Table of Contents and any links are working properly.

It's a lot easier and quicker to make changes to your book now, rather than waiting until after it's been published to KDP!

1.	Go to **https://www.amazon.com/gp/feature.html?ie=UTF8&docId=1000765261** and download the latest version of Kindle Previewer. Follow the instructions to install the software.

2.	Open your formatted MS Word manuscript and select "Save As" to save the document as a "Web Page, Filtered" (for PC) or "Web Page" (for Mac).

3.	Open the Previewer and then open your filtered web page. Previewer converts your web file to Kindle format.

4.	Click on "Preview Options," then select "Device Type" to preview it in several different Kindle viewers.

5 PUBLISHING YOUR EBOOK

Once you've formatted your MS Word file using the guidelines in Chapter 4, saved it as an HTML file, and checked the layout using Kindle Previewer, you're ready to publish!

We have included instructions for publishing to KDP, but most publishing platforms will follow a similar procedure, involving entering information about your book, selecting payment options, and downloading your file.

When you upload your HTML file to KDP (and other platforms), you'll need to make key decisions about how much you want to charge for your book and what genre(s) it fits into. These are important choices that will dramatically affect your sales, so it pays to consider them before you publish!

How to Publish

The process of publishing your eBook on Amazon KDP is easy. It's really a self-guided process. The sections and fields are labeled and explained in easy-to-understand language. Here, we have simplified it even more.

1. First, log into your KDP account or create one at https://kdp.amazon.com/en_US/

2. After signing in, you'll see your Book Shelf page. At the top in the "Create a New Title" section, click on "+Kindle eBook."

3. Fill out the fields of the "Kindle eBook Details" page. On this page, you'll give the title, author name(s), description, and other information that relates to your book. After filling out the title, author name, description, and categories, click "Save and Continue."

4. On the "Kindle eBook Content" page, fill out the KDP Select and Digital Right Management (DRM) information and upload the manuscript file. On this page, you will also either upload your cover file or create a cover using the Cover Creator. Click "Launch Cover Creator" to create a cover.

5. Now, click "Launch Previewer" to start the review process. This will show you what your book will look like as an eBook.

6. Fill out the Kindle eBook ISBN number if you have one. But this is optional. You do not have to have an ISBN number to publish an eBook.

7. You can fill in the name of your publisher if you want to, but that's also optional.

8. The last section, "Kindle eBook Pricing," pops up next. In this section, select KDP Select enrollment if you wish to do so. This will allow you to use free promotions on Amazon every 90 days. You'll get 5 free giveaway book days during this period. You can also choose the schedule a countdown discount if you wish to do so.

9. Now, you'll fill out the Royalty and Pricing section. If your book is $2.99 and above, then you will receive a 70% royalty. If your price is

below $2.99, then you'll receive only 35%.

10. When you've completed this page, click "Publish Your Kindle eBook."

11. Then click on "Go to My Bookshelf" to see a summary of your eBook information. The status should read "In Review." Later, it will say "Publishing," and when your book is finally published, it will say, "Live."

It takes Amazon between 12-48 hours to publish your book, but sometimes it's quicker than that. Although your book may appear in the Kindle Store, it won't be available for purchase until it's completely finished publishing.

NOTE: If at any time you get confused, click "Save and Continue" (to ensure you don't lose any information you've already entered) and then click "Help" at the top-right corner of the screen. Then look for your topic on the menu on the left side of the screen.

Making Changes and Updates in KDP

After your book is finished publishing to the Kindle Store, you can go into your KDP account at any time to make changes to your ebook or any of the information (pricing, rights, etc...) regarding it. For example, if you realize that your Table of Contents isn't working properly, or you spot a typo in your book, you can make changes to your MS Word file, then re-save it as a filtered web page to be re-published.

Editing Your Book on KDP

1. Log into your account on Amazon's Kindle Direct Publishing website at https://kdp.amazon.com/self-publishing/signin

2. Your Bookshelf will appear with a list of the book(s) you've uploaded and published to KDP. Beside each book title, you'll see a check box.

Click the box for the book you want to edit.

3. Now click on the grey "Actions" button. A drop-down menu appears. From that menu, select the action you wish to take. For example: "Edit book details" or "Edit rights, royalty and pricing."

4. If you want to upload a new version of your manuscript to KDP, simply select "Upload your book file," choose your file using the browse function and click "Save and Continue" at the bottom.

5. Click "Go To My Bookshelf" to see a summary of your ebook information. The status will read "Publishing."

NOTE: Do not select "Unpublish" from the "Actions" menu. If you do, your book will no longer be available on Kindle Select, and you'll have to republish it, which means entering all the same information over again and waiting for Amazon to review your book once again!

Pricing Your ebook

Here's the deal on pricing your ebook for Amazon Kindle... If you price your book below $2.99, you will not receive the 70 percent royalty on sales; you'll only receive 35 percent. So, if you only charge 99 cents per copy, you're going to receive 35 cents in royalties.

It's not a bad idea to start off low if this is your first book and you want to gain reviews and build up momentum for your book. But I would charge at least $1.99. You'll receive 70 cents, but that's a lot better than 35 cents!

Many new authors are charging $2.99 and holding their own on the charts, so pricing is really something that you should experiment with. I've found that my book sells well at $1.99. Later on, if it gains sales momentum, I'll up the price to $2.99 and see what happens.

Many people act as though "price cycling" is some anomaly. It's not. It's just testing out one price and then another to find your book's sweet spot. My book's sweet spot seems to be $1.99. I tried 99 cents and found that even fewer people bought it than when it was at $2.99.

Look at successful authors in your genre. How much are they selling and at what price? Today, many authors are choosing $1.99 and above, rather than 99 cents as in the past. Other popular price points are $3.99 and $4.99.

Here's a summary:

- **99 cents** = 35 cents for you at 35 percent royalty (because you priced below $2.99)
- **$1.99** = 70 cents for you at 35 percent royalty (still priced below $2.99)
- **$2.99** = $2.04 for you at 70 percent royalty

Using Categories to Sell Your Ebook

You've just uploaded your novel to Amazon's Kindle Direct Publishing and they e-mailed you back saying that it's now live on the Kindle Store. Don't breathe a sigh of relief just yet. Your book is in the store, but so are millions of other ebooks that your novel must compete with for readers' attention. How will they find your novel among the thousands of others in its category?

First of all, you need to experiment with the categories that your novel or book may fall into. For example, *House of Mirrors* is a cross-genre novel that can fall within the following genres: suspense, horror, thriller, and maybe even romance. So, the first few months of having my book on Amazon's website, I experimented by placing it in different genre categories to see how it fared. It didn't fare well in the extremely competitive romance category, but I kind of expected that. It did okay in the thriller and suspense categories, but it found its sweet spot in the Horror/Ghosts subcategory where it lives right now.

Here's a link to Amazon's list of subjects/genres, so you can see what's out there: **http://www.amazon.com/-/b/?node=1000.**

Click on the genre that best describes your work, and another page will open with subcategories (in the left column) and the number of titles in each category. You'll notice, when you try to select subcategories for your own book in KDP, that not all subcategories are available – reportedly, Amazon "saves" these for big-time authors whose publishing houses can afford to spend on marketing!

Changing Categories

You can easily move your novel or book into another category by logging into your Bookshelf on the KDP site. Here are the steps:

1. Log into your account on Amazon's KDP website at **https://kdp.amazon.com/self-publishing/signin**

2. Your Bookshelf will appear with a list of the book(s) you've uploaded and published to KDP. Beside each book title, you'll see a check box. Click the box for the book you want to edit.

3. Now click on the grey "Actions" button. A drop-down menu appears. From that menu, select "Edit eBook Details."

4. The book details page appears. Scroll down to Number 3 "Target Your Book to Customers" and click on "Add Categories."

5. Click the box beside the old categories that you want to delete. Once you click the old categories, they disappear from the box on the right.

6. Now, click the boxes beside the new categories you wish to select. They show up in the category box on the right.

7.   "Save and Publish." You're finished! It may take up to 12 hours for the changes to take place, but most likely it will only take around two hours.

NOTE: In order to list your title in certain sub-categories, you'll need to add Search Keywords. In the box directly under "Add Categories," type keywords that relate to your book. For example, if your book is Romance and it takes place during the holidays, you would select the categories FICTION>ROMANCE and then type into the Search Keywords box "Holiday."

Taking Advantage of Subcategories

Another tip about categorizing your book is to pay attention to how big each category and subcategory is. For instance, the Romance category under Amazon ebooks has more than 20,000 titles. That's a lot of books to compete against, but your book may stand up to the challenge, so go ahead if you think it may fall into that category. But also take a look at the smaller subcategories beneath that one.

Subcategories such as African American Women's Fiction (more than 10,000) under Literature & Fiction, and the subcategory Folk Tales under Mythology & Folk Tales (431) have less books with which to compete. Why is this important? The smaller the category, the easier it is for your book to rank high in that category and to show up on the first few pages of the Best Sellers list. In other words, it may only take a handful of sales to show up in the top 100 books for that specific category.

Sometimes, after you've gotten a huge number of downloads due to your free promo days on Kindle Select, you can tap out on that specific audience. So, what you'll want to do if you see sales waning is to change your book's category.

Let's say my book *House of Mirrors* has been in the Horror/Occult subcategory for a while now and my book was downloaded by thousands. The sales this time around aren't as good as they were when I did my first free promo event, so I switch the book to a new category like Mystery/Suspense or Horror/Ghosts. This may build my sales momentum back up. Try it! It's easy to switch categories.

6 THE PRE-LAUNCH

Once you've published your ebook, you may way to crack open a bottle of champagne and celebrate the fact that you're now a published author! But before you get too excited, you need to take a few steps to ensure that the public can actually find your book in order to purchase it!

You'll need to:
- set up a media kit (also called a Press Kit)
- create an author's page on Author Central (or equivalent publishing websites)
- Create a blog and/or author website
- Create social media accounts and learn to use hashtags and keywords

Before you dive in, think about this... The best way to launch a new book is to gradually release information about your book – don't release all of your blog announcements, tweets, Facebook posts, and mailing list/newsletter e-mails all in one day. Amazon's algorithm is set to target books with one-day surges in sales as fraudulent, and this could cause your book to be purposely ranked lower.

Amazon does this in order to prevent authors from

getting all of their friends and families to buy their book at once which, of course, would send their book racing to the top of the charts. As a result, the algorithm favors books with ongoing sales or growing sales.

In other words, gradual growth is good. So instead of blabbing news of your book's launch all in one day, why not blab first on your mailing list, then Twitter, and then the others over the course of three days? This sounds counterintuitive and lazy, but it helps. I wish I had done this when I released *House of Mirrors*.

Creating a Media Kit

A media kit is a packet of information about you and your book. You should have your kit available on a moment's notice – both in digital and print form, ideally – in case you happen to stumble upon a bookstore, an agent or editor, your local librarian, etc… That way, instead of raving on and on about your book, you can simply hand them your media kit! (Plus, you will seem very professional!)

A media kit should include the following information:

Bio – As a rough guide, your bio should be 100-200 words and should pertain to some aspect of your book. For example, if you are writing a supernatural thriller, you would want to mention that you're a member of the local ghost hunting group! Also mention any key writing credentials (a degree, a certificate, courses you've taken) and if you have won any awards (even if you don't think it's a big deal, an award is an award!). And write it in the third person, as though you are already famous!

Contact Information – At a minimum, list your email address. If you have a blog related to your writing/book, list that, as well as any social media (twitter, Facebook, Instagram, etc…) that are relevant.

Photographs – You will want to include a photograph of yourself, as well as an image of your book cover. Some authors get a professional photographer to take their photo, but this is up to you. Others get a friend or spouse to take a photograph – the best ones seem to be taken outside because the light is better!

Book Information – Give a brief summary of what your book is about – much like a pitch letter to an agent, keep it short! Give the full title of your book, your name, when the book was published, the name of the publisher, the genre and age range (if it's for kids or teens), the ISBN, where readers can find the publication, and where booksellers could order more of them. Include a photo of the cover.

Book Excerpt – This is optional, in my opinion. Like a resume, media kits shouldn't be too long. Two or three pages is an ideal length. You want to give a snapshot of yourself and your book.

Blurbs, Reviews, Endorsements – If you have some amazing blurbs from well-known authors, by all means include them, either on a separate page or in your "Book information" page.

Sample Author Q&A/Tip Sheet – This is another optional item. Some experts suggest including a list of commonly asked questions, such as "Where did you get the idea for your book?" for media interviews. In my experience, reporters already have a pretty good idea of the questions they want to ask! And a lot of the Q&A information could be included in the press release.

Press or News Release – This is basically a mini article about why your book is unique. Press releases are less relevant for authors today because we are more likely to announce our books on social media and other online platforms, rather than newspapers. Still, it's a good idea to have a press release available, even if you decide not to include it with your media kit. (See the section below on press releases for more details about how to write one.)

The bottom line?

Your media kit will be unique, like your book! Some media kits combine several types of information on one page – the book information, author's bio and photographs. Others use separate pages for the book information, Q&A, and excerpts. In the end, it's up to you. It's a good idea to check other author's media kits to see examples of how they format theirs.

Press release

Press releases, or news releases, are articles that you send (email or snail mail or fax) to media outlets to announce your book's release. The press then use your release as a basis to create a longer article with more in-depth information.

You can hire a marketing professional to write a press release for you, or you can write your own. The main things to remember about writing a press release are:
- Have a catchy "hook" in the first paragraph – It's not enough to simply announce that you've published a book. People publish ebooks every day. What's unique about your story? Are you writing from a fresh perspective? Do you cover an under-appreciated historical time period? Are you a regional writer who's stepping outside your comfort zone (perhaps trying science fiction)?
- Keep it short – two pages maximum.
- Don't forget to include contact information so that media outlets can reach you!!
- Distribute widely – You can send your press release to specific media outlets (online magazines, print

venues, blogs, etc...), but you'll need to make sure you send it to the right contact people. This requires research and time. A free PR service will send out your press release for you to multiple locations, but the distribution may not be as focused as a paid service.

Optimize Author Central on Amazon

If you've published your book via KDP, sign up for Author Central to set up an Author's Page, where you manage your public profile, check your sales rank (see later section), and create a book description for your book's product page that includes bolded headings and key points to make it really stand out! You can't do that if you use only KDP for your book's description.

Here's how to sign up:
1. Go to Author Central at **http://authorcentral.amazon.com** and click "Join Now."
2. Sign in using your Amazon email address and password.
3. Read the Author Central's Terms and Conditions, and then click "Agree" to accept them.
4. Enter the name your book is written under. A list of possible book matches appears.
5. Select your book.
6. Click "Profile" at the top of the page to enter your profile information. Some features will not be available right away (it takes Amazon a day or two to create your Author's Page).

Once Amazon has created your Author Page, use it to connect all your social media. From the "Profile" page, you can link to your blog and Twitter account so that readers will see the latest updates. You can also post photographs of yourself and add videos, such as your book trailers and author readings and interviews. And you can list any upcoming author's events, such as blog tours, which we'll cover in a later section.

Creating Your Author URL

Author Central lets you create a short, easy-to-use URL that links directly to your Author Page. You can cut and paste this short URL whenever you want to share your Author Page on Twitter, your blog, Facebook, or any social media site. You can also add it to the bottom of your outgoing emails as part of your "signature."

1. Sign into your Author Central Account.
2. Click on "Profile" at the top of the page.
3. On the right-hand side of the page, you'll see the words "Author Page URL." Click "add link."
4. Amazon will suggest a URL for you (for example, http://www.amazon.com/author/louisadang), but you can customize it if you like. If that URL isn't available, you'll have to come up with another one. Choose carefully because once you create your URL, you'll have to go through Customer Service to change it!

Optimizing Your Book Description

It's easy to make changes to your Author Page and to customize your book description.

1. Log in to Author Central.
2. Click on "Books" from the navigation bar at the top of the screen.
3. Click on your book title. A page will appear with information about your book. By clicking on the "Editorial Reviews" tab, you can edit several features of the book, like the book's description.
4. Find "Product Description" and click "Edit." This takes you to an editor box. Remember,

your Author Central book description will trump the one you uploaded in Kindle Direct Publishing, so the book description in Author Central will be the one your customers will see on your book's product page on Amazon.

5. If you don't know HTML, then click the "Compose" tab of the editor box. Here, you can make changes and bold words (highlight whatever you want to put in bold and then click the "B" key for bold).

6. When you are finished, click "Preview." If your description looks good, click "Save changes."

Sound simple? It is. Your changes in Author Central should take effect within 10 minutes to several hours, but it's much faster than changes made using KDP only.

Using Your ASIN to Your advantage!

If you'd like to promote your book on your website or blog, you'll definitely want to insert some links to it on the Kindle Store if that's where it's published. While you can use your Author Central URL to link to your Author Page on Amazon, you can also create an easy-to-use link to your book's specific product page.

Create a direct link to your book's detail page from other websites by adding your 10-character Amazon Standard Identification Number to the end of the URL below, in place of the letters ASIN:

http://www.amazon.com/dp/ASIN

You can find your ASIN under the book's title in your KDP Bookshelf or on the book's detail page under "Product Details." You can include this link inside the Kindle version of your book as well.

Amazon allows you to use their trademarks or logos to advertise your book on another website, as long as you follow the Kindle Brand Use Guidelines (http://amzn.to/14q85n8) and use approved logos.

Creating Websites and Blogs

If you are fairly good with technical stuff, you can create a free website using WordPress software. Go to **http://www.wordpress.org**, where you can download and install the free software script. You'll need a web host who meets the minimum requirements, and you'll need to read the instructions on the website, as there's a lot to learn. But once you know how to customize it, WordPress is an excellent tool for creating professional-looking websites.

However, if you have minimal technical skills, you may want to set up a free WordPress-based blog in seconds. Go to **http://wordpress.com**. It's much easier than downloading the software and has lots of templates, but it can't do as much as the WordPress software you download and install yourself.

For less than $10 per year, you can change the URL of your blog from "wordpress.com" to simply "yourwebsite.com." This looks more like a website, rather than a free blog! You can also pay to upgrade your blog to "Premium." This adds more features to your WordPress site – such as the ability to add video and monetizing your site.

Google blogs

You can make an even easier-to-use blog using Google's **blogger.com**. It is a little more basic than WordPress, but it has lots of templates for you to choose from and still looks professional and has widgets to connect with your Facebook and Twitter accounts.

Another site to check out is **weebly.com**, which offers free websites and blogs. We haven't used this site but know people who have, successfully. Others have also used wix.com, which has gotten good reviews on the site **https://superbwebsitebuilders.com**/ This site gives good overviews of popular website-building services.

To maximize your online exposure, create multiple blogs and try out each of these formats to see which one you like best. For example, you could have a blog that focuses on your book, another that talks about you as an author, and a third for a related topic that you are passionate about and you know will be interesting to your readers.

Write for your target audience – your readers! Who are they? How old are they? What gender? What topics do they want to read about?

To save time, you can repurpose blog content and use it on multiple sites. Try to post updates to your blog at least once a week to keep readers interested. And link your blogs to all your other forms of social media: your website, Twitter, Facebook, Amazon, etc...

Maximizing Key Words

A good way to drive more traffic to your blog is to sprinkle in popular keywords throughout your blog postings and website content. The first 100 words of your blog postings should contain high traffic keywords.

I have found that it's best to choose keywords that aren't necessarily the top most popular ones for my topic. The reason is that those keywords are already pretty much taken over by the big honchos of the industry. For instance, if I was selling my suspense novel, I wouldn't want to choose the top keyword "suspense" because you know someone like James Patterson is all over that one.

The first few pages of the Google search results obviously are going to show the top suspense authors. In other words, there's very little chance that you will end up on the first few pages of search results for "suspense." I would rather choose something like "suspense novelists in NC" or "Southern suspense" or "paranormal suspense novels."

You can find popular keywords for your topic by using the following tools and websites:

Google Trends - http://www.google.com/trends

This is where you can find a list of the searches that have the most traffic on an hourly basis. You can also study search patterns by location, which is helpful for writers targeting their local audience as well as national and international ones.

Keyword Explorer - https://moz.com/explorer

You can set up a free Moz account and try this service and other marketing tools free for 30 days. After that, prices start at $99 per month ($79 if you pay yearly). So, take advantage of the free month because Moz has some great tools!

Activate Backlinks

Backlinks (also called "pingbacks," "trackbacks" or "linkbacks") let you keep track of other pages on the web that have linked back to your blog posts. This way, you can see who's interested in what you have to say. You can then make comments on their blogs and build new contacts.

Another good reason to activate the backlinks feature on your blog is that the more links connecting to your website, the higher your Google ranking, which means it is easier for people to find you and your books.

According to most search engine experts, Google gives higher value to backlinks that cover the same topics. So, find blogs and websites in your area of expertise and post comments and offer to write guest posts. Then, in your bio or somewhere in the content, link back to your blog.

For most blogs, it's easy to activate the backlinks feature. Here are instructions how to do it in WordPress.com:

http://en.support.wordpress.com/comments/trackbacks/

Some sites automatically activate backlinks, so check the settings for posts and comments in whatever web platform you are using.

7 LAUNCH YOUR BOOK AND TRACK YOUR SUCCESS

Okay, you have your published book, your blog or website set up for your book with links to your media kit, and you've set up author's pages on Amazon, Goodreads, and other relevant sites where readers can purchase your book. You're ready for the official launch!

What is a launch? It's basically the time you present your book to the world. So, start sending out the announcements that your book is ready and waiting!

Cashing in on Your Sales Rank!

Once you start selling, you need to keep track of your sales! There are two main rankings people talk about when they talk about Amazon – the recommendation system and the sales rank.

Recommendations are the books that appear on just about every page of Amazon Books: "More to Explore" and "More Items to Consider" and "Customers who bought this item also bought..." They're the book covers displayed under the different genres. For example, under

"Mystery & Thrillers," Stephen King's *Joyland* is listed.

These categories are based on factors like what books customers have previously bought, which books they have "Liked" and reviewed, and a whole host of other things that are known only to Amazon. If your book is recommended by Amazon, fantastic! The rest of us mortals must rely on something we can control – sales rank.

Your sales rank is earned simply by sales alone. If an Amazon Prime Member borrows your book from the Kindle Owner's Lending Library, that counts as a sale. If you gift your book to a friend, that counts as a sale as soon as the recipient approves and accepts the gift. A free download does not affect the paid sales rank but does affect the free sales rank at the time of a free promo day.

The lower your sales rank, the more books you are selling. So, a book ranked #1 is the top-selling book at that moment. A book ranked 4 million is not doing too well! Sales ranks are constantly changing, but if your book is consistently in the top 1000, that's pretty darn good!

Making the Best Seller Lists

Boosting your sales rank improves your chances of getting on one of Amazon's Kindle Best Sellers lists, which means amazing exposure! To see some examples of current best sellers:

1. Go to Amazon Books (**http://amzn.to/13KHASe**).
2. In the left-hand column, click on Kindle ebooks.
3. When the Kindle ebooks page appears, look in the left-hand column and click on Kindle Best Sellers.
4. When the "Best Sellers" page appears, look to the right-hand of the screen for the words "See more." Click on that link.
5. The next page will show two tabs – "Top 100 Paid" and "Top 100 Free."

When you see someone's overall Amazon Best Sellers Rank at around 1,000, that means that person is selling around 90-100 books per day. If the overall Amazon Best Sellers Rank is #1-5, then that author is selling around 3,000 or more books per day.

Here's a link to a sales rank calculator that tells you roughly how many books you are selling per day, based on your sales rank:

https://kindlepreneur.com/amazon-kdp-sales-rank-calculator/

Gifting Your Book = Better Ranking

Do gifted books count as sales? Yes! But they don't count for "Amazon Verified Purchase" reviews (this confirms that the person reviewing your book purchased it on Amazon). The more books you have gifted, the higher your sales ranking anyway.

One way to increase your ranking via gifting is to temporarily change your book's price to 99 cents if it's not already that price. Then gift several copies to family and friends, and it will only cost you around $20 or so for 20 gifts. Once the receiver accepts and opens your gift, it counts as a sale on Amazon.

Giving it Away for Free

The best benefit for independent authors in the KDP Select program is the five-day free promotion period every 90 days. During your free promotion days, Amazon will promote your book on their site and offer it for free on the days you select.

You may think giving away your book for free is a waste of your time and possibly a loss in future sales but think again. Many have reaped benefits of higher rankings on Amazon, placement on best seller lists, and an increase in sales after a Kindle Select free days event.

Making the Most of Kindle Select's Free Promo Days

You can either use all five days consecutively or you can schedule them sporadically throughout the 90-day period. Used correctly, you'll see your sales rank jump sky-high, and you'll get great exposure on the Kindle ebooks Top 100 Free Best Sellers list!

Most people choose to have a two- or three-day free event rather than just one day. One day is not enough to pull high ranking in the best seller lists for the appropriate genre in which you choose to assign your book. Five days is too long. Most people find that interest wanes after the second or third day.

For my novel *House of Mirrors*, the interest waned after the second day. My book started dropping down the best seller lists. Your book may be more interesting and may keep a higher rank for a longer period of time. It's a matter of testing the market with each free promo event you do.

Free downloads don't count toward sales rank, but still sometimes it only takes about 20-50 downloads in one day to reach the top ten of a subgenre's best seller list. The most important benefit is that a free promo can encourage word-of-mouth marketing of your book and if enough people buy your book, the Amazon algorithm will start recommending your book.

Setting Up a Free Promo

In order to run a free promo event on Amazon, you must first enroll your book in KDP Select. When you upload your book to Amazon's Kindle Direct Publishing platform, you'll see an option for enrolling your book in Kindle Select. Just check that box.

The following is a brief step-by-step guide for setting up your free promotion days:

1. Log into your account on Amazon's Kindle Direct Publishing (KDP) website at https://kdp.amazon.com/self-publishing/signin
2. You'll see your "Bookshelf," or a list of the book(s) you've uploaded and published to KDP.
3. In your Bookshelf, click "Promote and Advertise" next to any book enrolled in KDP Select.
4. Choose "KDP Select Info."
5. Under "Run a Price Promotion," select "Free Book Promotion."
6. Click "Create a new Free Book Promotion Deal" for this book.
7. Fill in the desired start and end date and click "Save." (You only get five days out of a 90-day period to run free promos. We generally run our first promos for two days, and six weeks later run our second promos for three days.)

Creating Hype for Free Promo Days

One major factor that will affect the success of your free promo days event is the pre-promo hype you create via social media. You need to spread the word by sending out ads, press releases, tweeting, posting on Facebook, and blogging about it. Many writers endure what's called a "blog tour" – we'll talk more about that in the blogging section.

Websites to advertise your Kindle Select free days

You can advertise your promo days ahead of time to let readers know to watch out for your book. Here are some websites that specialize in helping authors advertise their free and low-cost ebooks. Some these are free, and others are fairly inexpensive.

Note: Some sites will not promote erotica.

http://www.indiesunlimited.com/ (This site also has a great list of book promotion websites.)
http://digitalbooktoday.com
http://worldliterarycafe.com (As of publication date, this site is under construction.)
http://bargainebookhunter.com
http://ereadernewstoday.com
http://kindlebookpromos.luckycinda.com
http://bookgoodies.com
http://www.fkbooksandtips.com
http://www.everythingbooksandauthors.com

The following website is a great resource to research paid and unpaid book promo sites:
https://blog.reedsy.com/book-promotion-services/

Track Your Sales Rank

In order to see if your blogging, tweeting, ads, and free promo days have been successful, you'll need to keep track of your sales rank. To do this, use your book's product page on Amazon. It's located under the "Product Details" section which is usually mid-page, above customer reviews.

- You can also check your KDP Sales Reports, which lists eight different kinds of reports, including your "Sales Dashboard."
- You can use a website called NovelRank.com (**http://www.novelrank.com**/). It's free and easy to use. Just copy and paste your Amazon URL in the field provided on the front page of NovelRank.com.
- Kindle Nation Daily's ebookTracker is worth checking out, especially if you'd like to track your competitors' books. You can track several books at one time and group them if you'd like. It's free, but you have to register. Here's the link: **http://tracker.kindlenationdaily.com**

Shine Online!

The more about you and your book online, the better. Blogs, websites, and social media tools like Twitter increase your web exposure, give readers a taste of your writing style, and help build a fan base for your books.

Blog Tours

Many authors do blog tours to increase their exposure. Unlike traditional book tours, where authors travel to different cities and states to give readings, online writers save time and money by "stopping by" high-traffic blogs to do a guest post, an interview, or perhaps just introduce themselves and their books and offer free copies.

Review blog tours are also popular – this is where the host blog reviews your book during your "stop." The only problem with this is that the reviewer is under no obligation to give you a positive review!

To set up a tour, you must first research blogs in your genre – ideally, high-traffic ones! But you also want to attract new readers from outside your niche, so try to include some more general-topic blogs as well. For example, if you have written a paranormal thriller that has elements of romance, you may also want to check out popular romance blogs. Or, perhaps a blog for ghost-hunting enthusiasts! Keep in mind, your goal is to attract readers who will want to buy your books, not just other writers!

Next, send out queries to host bloggers to set up a schedule of "stops" and agree on what you'll write about. Then, write your blog posts ahead of time, so you'll be prepared on the day. Tours could last anywhere from five days to a month, depending on your stamina!

Because blog tours are so draining, some writers hire companies to set up the stops and do all the leg-work for them. If you do hire a blog tour company, be sure to ask to see examples of previous tours they've set up – check that the blogs are reputable and visible. You can also check the blogs' traffic by using sites like StatShow (**http://www.statshow.com**), or by simply looking at the number of followers and comments a blogger has.

Some writers are choosing to do "live" tours, using Twitter or other social media tools in a question-and-answer format. These require less writing ahead of time but can be just as exhausting!

Tweet Like Crazy!

While some argue that writers should spend more time writing and less time tweeting, Twitter is a great tool to help you gain exposure for your blog, connect with other writers and professionals in the industry, and spread the word about your books. So, why not give it a try?

Tweet Teams

If you would like to increase your following on Twitter, a great way to do that is via tweet teams. Tweet teams are groups of people (writers in this case) who retweet each other's tweets in order to boost followership and gain exposure for their books.

Scheduling Tweets

You may be asking, "How do I schedule tweets?" The two most popular tweet schedulers are TweetDeck (**http://tweetdeck.com**/) and HootSuite (**https://hootsuite.com**/). We prefer HootSuite, but we know of many who sing the praises of TweetDeck. Try both. They're fairly easy.

HootSuite allows you to schedule Facebook and other social media posts and messages as well as Twitter tweets. You write your message or tweet at the top left-hand field box and click on the tiny calendar icon in the right-hand side of the field box. A calendar appears where you'll choose the date and time at which you would like the tweet or post released to your followers or Facebook friends. Select the date and time and click OK. Your tweets will be sent out at the specified days and times.

Here's a great article that lists more popular free and low-cost tweet schedulers: **https://writtent.com/blog/best-twitter-scheduling-tools/**

Check out Chapter 8 for information about using hashtags in Twitter

Mailing Lists: If you build it, they will come

Mailing lists may be the most underused and underestimated marketing tool for writers. Why? They can really help out when you release your new book. Having a group of readers know about your new release at the same time and acting upon it could place your book among Amazon's Hot New Releases. The more reader e-mails you collect, the more your sales momentum should increase.

One of the best methods for collecting reader e-mails is by using the back matter of your ebook. After the story ends, that's when you include a short note or link to your mailing list where readers can be the first to know when your new books are released. This gives the reader a sense of being "in the know," and it also maintains an ongoing relationship with that customer.

It's also a good idea to post sign-up links for your new release mailing list on blogs and social media sites. Some authors entice their readers to sign up for their mailing lists by giving away something for free like a short story, or they offer special discounts on their ebooks.

Whatever you do, make sure you are in full compliance with CAN-SPAM legislation, which sets the rules for commercial email. You can't add people to your mailing list without their permission. Here's a link for more information: http://1.usa.gov/13PBzKQ

Do I Need an email marketing list provider?
Providers help you gather email addresses of readers who want to subscribe to your blog or receive your email updates. They can provide you with a customized sign-up form (saving you the trouble of creating one!) and can also send out automatic responses to all your subscribers.

Many providers will also let you "segment" your addresses into different categories – such as by location or age or gender, depending on who you're trying to target with specific messages. They'll also track how many readers actually open your emails.

These are three popular mailing list providers:

- **Mail Chimp (http://mailchimp.com/)** – Free for up to 2,000 email subscribers but doesn't have all the bells and whistles of paid services. Paid plans start at only $10 per month.
- **Aweber (http://www.aweber.com)** – One of the most popular providers. It has lots of features and great customer support. Prices start at $19 per month for up to 500 subscribers.
- **Constant Contact (https://www.constantcontact.com)** – A very popular provider. The first 60 days are free, and then plans start at $20 per month for up to 500 subscribers. Like most plans, you save money if you pay annually, rather than monthly.

Here's a great overview of the top 7 email marketing services: http://www.wpbeginner.com/showcase/best-email-marketing-services/

Book Reviews

First of all, book reviews do not affect Amazon's algorithm; therefore, don't expect the number of book reviews you have to catapult your visibility on Amazon.

However, what counts here are positive reviews. This gives a customer reassurance that you're the real thing; you're not just a hack churning out garbage. Book reviews, of course, work as a two-edged sword. A negative review can sink your star ranking and turn away future customers.

In the last few years, Amazon has been criticized for deleting reviews or of not posting them at all. This is because Amazon changed its review policy to weed out paid-for, fake reviews. What does this mean for you? Well, while you may be tempted to hit up all your friends and family for reviews of your book, stick with the ones who are less active on social media. Amazon checks your social media connections and may delete reviews by family members and those they deem to be close connections.

Also, if you are selling your book on Amazon, be careful about connecting with your favorite authors on social media, such as Twitter. Follow their posts but don't necessarily "friend" them or link to them. If you decide to ask them for a review, Amazon may decide that they are too close of a connection and not publish their review!

But don't worry! You can always join author book review groups on Goodreads (**http://www.goodreads.com/group**) to link up with readers you don't personally know. This is an excellent way to gather and trade honest reviews with other authors and readers. Another idea is to post a request for reviews in exchange for a free book on a forum such as KBoards (**http://www.kboards.com/**).

Writing reviews of other authors' books, especially those in the same genre of your own, is another way to spread the word about your book. If you do write reviews, make sure you write professionally without mistakes. Customers will judge you by those and it may turn them off immediately. Additionally, the more you review, the higher your ranking as a reviewer on Amazon will rise. You can gain some exposure by this, but it will take time and plenty of reviews.

When Bad Reviews Happen to Good Writers...

If you receive negative reviews, don't respond to them. In fact, I wouldn't respond to any review, positive or negative, because it can work against you. You can always privately e-mail a reviewer and thank them that way, rather than publicly.

The reason you shouldn't respond to negative reviews is because it puts you in a bad light and invites trouble-making reviewers to seek revenge upon you. Reviewers gossip among each other about authors who are sore losers and that can lead to a bunch of them ganging up on your book.

Group Promotions

You and your author friends can combine efforts on social media to sell books as a group promotion. This has proven very effective for many ebook authors, and it's fairly easy to carry out. All you need are friends who sell on Kindle Select, free promo days, and a little extra effort from each group member to get the word out.

First of all, gather other writers preferably in the same genre and give your group promotion a catchy name. Create a graphic banner for your blog post or social media entries, advertising your group promotion. Try to make the promo enticing and of value. For instance, you can combine the amount of money all your books normally cost and say, "Get $50 worth of books for free today through Wednesday!"

All of the members of the group promo should schedule their Kindle Select free promo days for the same dates and combine their efforts to get the word out via social media and blog posts. Include links to your books, of course.

8 HASHTAG HELP FOR AUTHORS

When I first heard the word "hashtag," I was like "Say what?" Visions of illegal bongs in a smoky den came to mind. Hash? But I quickly learned that what I used to call the "pound sign" on the phone is now on social media platforms referred to as the "hashtag." It's one of the most useful tools for having your work discovered online. Here's how you use it to promote your book…

You can use the hashtag on the most popular social media networks such as Facebook, Twitter, Instagram, Google+, and Pinterest. It's a way of categorizing content on these social media platforms. The hashtag makes your content discoverable to the search engine bots and of course the users in search of your type of content.

By "content" I mean your blog, books ads, and of course your ebook or book. The hashtag allows you to interact with other social media users about a common topic or theme and it allows you to interact with a targeted audience across social media platforms.

Knowing how to use and manipulate hashtags can help move your book title up in search engine ranking and expose it to more readers. Here are a few tips we've learned along the way…

The Basics First…

Hashtags are like a shortcut on your computer desktop. They act as a shortcut to a group of likeminded people searching for the same topic. This is your targeted audience. That's why hashtags are so powerful. Instead of casting a net out to the blue yonder of the Internet, you're casting the net out to a specific pool of people. A hashtag is a pound sign (#) plus the keyword or tag.

That's basically it, but if you would like a more exhaustive explanation and guide to hashtags, check out Hootsuite's guide on using hashtags.

Hashtags for Marketing Your ebook

#bookgiveaway: Exactly what it says. You're giving your book away as a free copy promotion or as a raffle or contest. Make sure to include the hashtag #Free to assure people that it is truly free.

#novelines: You can use this one for quotes from your book or from others.

#poetrymonth: April is National Poetry Month, so this is a great hashtag to use if you're a poet.

#shortreads: Short stories. Don't forget May is National Short Story Month!

#teasertuesday and **#samplesunday**: Here you can offer a sample chapter of your work-in-progress. You may end up getting some great advice about how to improve it before publishing. Readers can easily find free chapters and excerpts with these two hashtags.

#indiethursday: Readers of independently published books tweet about their "indie" purchases here on Thursday of course.

Other Popular Hashtags

- ✓ **#mswl: Manuscript Wishlist**. This is very helpful if you are searching for an agent or editor who is in search of a specific type of manuscript. They may be looking for one like yours!
- ✓ **#amwriting.** A place where you can boast or complain about your latest greatest work.
- ✓ **#amediting.** A place to ask for suggestions on a clip of your work-in-progress or to chat or curse about the revision process.
- ✓ **#writingtip or #writetip.** You can find writing tips from other authors here or offer some of your own.
- ✓ **#writingprompt**
- ✓ **#nanowrimo.** National Novel Writing Month (November)
- ✓ **#writerwednesday.** Author promotion purposes
- ✓ **#fridayreads.** To support other writers' works. Good karma y'all.
- ✓ **#ff.** Friday Follow. Weekly show of Twitter generosity.
- ✓ **#book**
- ✓ **#novel**
- ✓ **#nonfiction**
- ✓ **#fiction or #fiction plus genre such as #womensfiction or #crime #fiction**
- ✓ **#paperback #paperbacks**
- ✓ **#new**
- ✓ **#special**
- ✓ **#free**
- ✓ **#bookbuzz**

Finding the Most Popular #Hashtags

Twitter lists some of the most popular hashtags trending for the day on the left-hand side of the Twitter home page screen of your profile page. These are great, but you may not want to use #iloveJustinBieber in your tweets about your latest novel. To find relevant and popular hashtags, you'll need to try the following sites.

Note: Most of these sites are free, but if you want more extensive data analysis, you have to pay for membership.

http://www.hashtags.org - Using this site is easy. Just type in the keywords (without spaces between the words if it's a phrase) in the search box in the top right-hand corner of the screen. Click "Enter," and the site will offer you information related to that keyword or hashtag for the past 24 hours. If you upgrade, you can view popularity graphs for the specific hashtag by time and day. Also, you'll find a list of related hashtags and the usernames of those who use them.

http://www.twazzup.com - You must sign into your Twitter account to access this tool. It provides real-time search info on hashtags. You will also find related hashtags and usernames of popular hashtags.

http://www.trendsmap.com - On the opening page, a visual map provides you the top trending Twitter topics for each part of the country. When you click on a word, a window with the top retweets opens. But for anything more than that, you have to pay for an account, starting at $25 per month.

http://www.twubs.com - This tool is great for networking as well as finding the most trending hashtags. You can join Twub groups related to a specific hashtag. And it's free!

All of these sites give you important historical data that you can use to decide whether or not a specific hashtag will tread water or not. The hashtags marked as spam show up at the bottom of the page which is also helpful in choosing the right hashtags for your tweets.

Another tip for finding the most popular hashtags and keywords for your tweets and blogs is to check out what the most popular ebook authors are using. Look up their profiles and blogs and see what keywords they use and how often they use them. You can find a list of best-selling Kindle authors on the Kboards website at **http://www.kboards.com/authors/**

9 USING METRICS AND ANALYTICS

What the heck are "metrics" and "analytics"? They are similar but not exactly the same. You can use metrics and analytics to understand which of your book marketing strategies are working and which ones aren't.

Metrics are actual numbers or data that you can collect, such as:
- How many people visited my author website last week?
- Which articles on my blog got the most views?
- Which Tweets were most often retweeted?
- What times of day are my Facebook followers most active?
- How many visitors clicked on the link for my ebook?
- Does Twitter or Facebook send the most traffic to my website?
- How many ebooks did I sell last week? This year?

Analytics is how you use this data to help you make the best marketing decisions. Using analytics, you can answer questions like:

- Which social media platform is the best to promote my book?
- How can I improve my blog readership by next month?
- Why is no one clicking on the link for my ebook?
- Why did I sell 20 books last month and only two this month?
- Should I spend more time blogging or more time Tweeting?
- Should I skip Facebook altogether?

For more in-depth information, this article gives a good explanation of the difference between metrics and analytics:
https://workforcedynamics.wordpress.com/2014/05/14/the-differences-between-metrics-and-analytics/

Don't Go Overboard!

There is so much data out there to collect that it's easy to spend hours a day scanning the number of people retweeting your Tweets or sharing your Facebook posts and wondering what to do with all that information. To avoid using up all your time and energy, start with your main goal and work from there.

Relevant metrics

Maybe your goal is to sell 10 books per week using the PayPal button on your website. You'll need to figure out what sort of data to track – in other words, what metrics will be most useful? You may want to track:

- Number of people each week who visit the page that has the PayPal button
- Number of these visitors who click on the button
- Number of clicks that lead to actual book sales
- Number of visitors who visit your blog each week that don't visit the PayPal button page

After collecting the relevant data, perhaps you found out that you had 27 visitors to your blog last week. But only one visited the page with the PayPal button, even though you have links everywhere to it. That one visit, however, resulted in a sale.

Time for analytics!

So, how can you make sure that all visitors are directed to the right page to buy your book? Once at the right page, will they buy your book? Or was it just dumb luck that one person actually stumbled upon the PayPal button and bought it?

Moving forward

Now, you have a place to start. You can try different strategies to direct visitors to your book page.

1. You try making the links more visible.
2. Then you gather information for one week – nope, this time no one reached the PayPal button page.
3. Maybe all the links scattered throughout your article are too distracting, and readers are losing interest. You take all the links out and place one prominent link at the end of your article.
4. You use metrics to see the results – success! Six people visited the PayPal page. Three of them bought your book!
5. Now, you know to cut down on the huge number of links and let visitors actually read the article! You also know that your PayPal button page is fairly successful.
6. Next goal – convert even more visits to book sales!

This is a basic example, but it gives you an idea of how you can use metrics and analytics to reach a specific goal – improving the flow of traffic on your website.

Google Analytics

Google Analytics is a tool that lets you track who is visiting your website, how they get there, and what links they click on once they arrive at your website. You can find out information like which social media channels are driving visitors to your website, what countries visitors live in, and which of your ads are generating revenue.

You create a free account, and then you are given a code to copy and paste into every web page you want to track. This sounds easy, but you are pasting HTML code, and you have to know exactly where to paste it.

Some free sites (such as WordPress.com) require a plugin to use Google Analytics, and for that you may need to pay a fee to upgrade.

This is an excellent article about how to set up and use Google Analytics: **https://moz.com/blog/absolute-beginners-guide-to-google-analytics**

All the Other Analytics Tools...

For someone less technically savvy who is using a free website or blog, Google Analytics may not be the way to go. Most social media tools, including Facebook, Twitter, and the free WordPress sites, include tools to track your visitors, followers, and basic information about them.

Facebook Insights

If you have set up a Facebook business page for your book, once you get 30 Likes, you automatically have access to Facebook Insights.

Here's an example from Louisa's Facebook page for her kids' magazine. Look on the top navigation bar for the "Insights" tab.

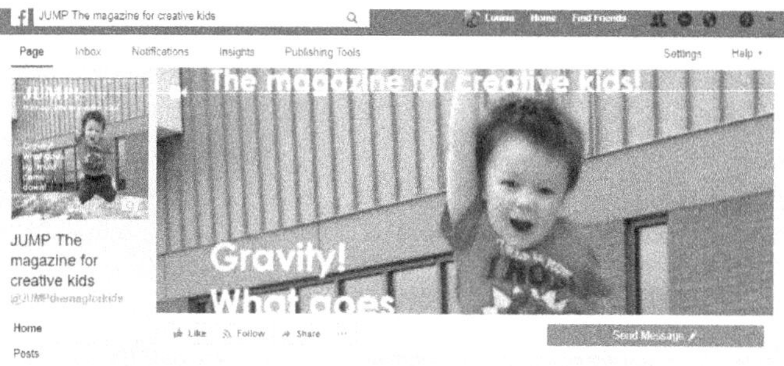

Here's what the page looks like once you click on "Insights."

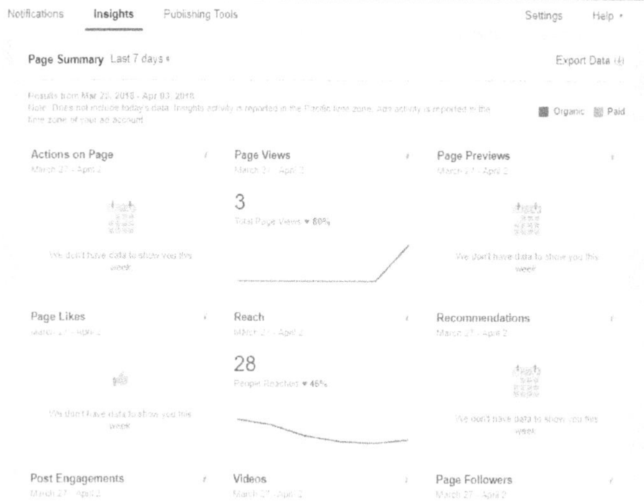

As you can see, Louisa's page is showing metrics from the past seven days. But you can change the range – to the current day or zoom out as far as the entire quarter. You can also select "custom" to look at a specific range of dates.

One of the most useful metrics to look at is "Post Engagements" (bottom-left of graphic). Click on this section to see the times of day when your page is the most active. So, for example, if you find out that most people are interacting with your page around 4 p.m. in the afternoon, you may want to start posting around that time to maximize your views.

You'll also find a listing of all your page posts, along with how many people interacted with the post – through likes, shares, and reactions. You can study which content was the most popular and try to duplicate those types of posts.

This article has a great overview of Facebook Insights and how to use it to your advantage: **https://blog.bufferapp.com/facebook-insights**

Twitter Analytics

If you use Twitter, be sure to check out their analytics tools. They are free and easy to access. First, you can look at the metrics for an individual tweet to see how many people have viewed it or clicked on it for more information.

Simply click on the icon that looks like three little lines at the bottom right of your tweet:

A window labeled "Tweet Activity" will open:

Tweet Activity

Louisa @LouisaDang	Impressions	710
JUMP! The magazine for creative kids!	Total engagements	5
https://issuu.com/southernbendmags/docs/spring_2018		
via @issuu	Likes	3
	Retweets	2

You'll be able to see how many times your tweet showed up in people's feeds – this is "Impressions." You can also see how many likes and retweets it received – "Total engagements." This is an easy way to check if a particular tweet (especially a pinned tweet) is piquing interest.

☐ Another great tool is **Twitter Analytics**. You find this by clicking on your profile picture at the top of the screen and selecting "Analytics."

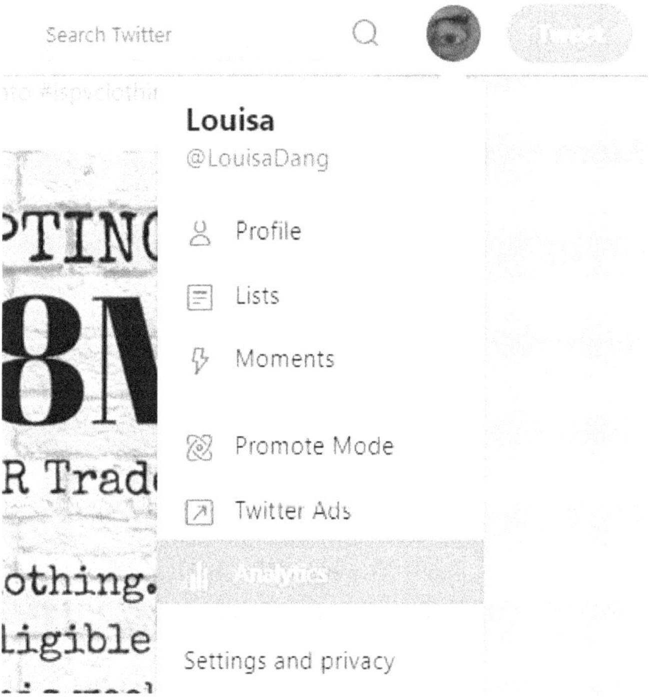

Twitter Analytics will tell you which tweets earned the most impressions and engagements in a given time period. The "Audiences" tab is helpful in seeing who is viewing and engaging with your tweets. You can find out your followers' top interests (such as politics and current events), gender, consumer behavior, and other details.

Knowing more about your audience helps you craft tweets to grab their attention! If your audience is primarily female, for example, and you want to increase male followers, experiment with different types of tweets -- add hashtags you think might appeal to a male audience. Then use Twitter Analytics to see what worked and what didn't.

You can even look at geographic regions to see which areas of the world your tweets are most popular! This comes in handy if you are trying to sell copies of your book in different languages.

This article gives a more in-depth look at how to use Twitter Analytics:
https://blog.bufferapp.com/twitter-analytics

More Free Analytics Tools...

Blogger and WordPress websites offer free analytics tools when you sign up with them. These free tools show metrics like how many people are visiting your site, which part of the world they live in, and how they reached your site (through Facebook, Twitter, etc…). There are also free link-shortening tools that offer great metrics.

Shorten and Track Your Links

By using a link-shortening service like **bitly.com**, you can track how many people click on important links, like your book product page. Not only does bitly abbreviate your website address, but it also tracks the shortened URLs for you after you post them to social media sites like Twitter, Facebook, etc...

For instance, if I tweet about my free promo coming up and insert the URL for my blog, abbreviated by bitly, I can later track that link to see if it was effective. This is another type of metrics you can use to find out which social media format works best for you.

This article gives an excellent overview of the top URL-shorteners and their associated analytics: **https://www.crazyegg.com/blog/url-shorteners-analytics/**

And to find more free analytics tools, simply do a Google search – this article lists some of the most popular free tools: **https://contently.com/strategist/2016/08/02/the-top-10-free-content-analytics-tools/**

10 QUESTIONS AND ANSWERS

In this section, we've compiled a list of some of the questions and issues we had when we were starting out as self publishers. Feel free to contact us via our websites (see our bios at the front of this book) if you have more questions, and we'll add them to our next edition!

Publishing ebooks Internationally

Will people in other countries be able to download my ebook for free on my Amazon promotional days?
Yes. Amazon has online stores all around the world in most countries. Just look at the bottom of your book's product page and you'll find a link to the international Amazon stores such as Amazon.ca (Canada), Amazon.de (Germany), Amazon.fr (France), etc. Click on the country's Amazon store and look up your book. You'll be able to see your book's product page for that specific country along with any reviews.

Will my ebook be immediately available on Amazon in other countries?
Yes, your book will be sold in all the Kindle stores in

which you have publishing rights. Unless you only hold rights for your work in certain countries, you should have checked "Worldwide rights – all territories" when you were publishing your book via KDP.

Do I still get paid in dollars?

Yes, Amazon will automatically move your earnings into your bank account by Electronic Funds Transfer (EFT). If you have sales from other countries, they will be converted into dollars. If you want to be paid by check or have the payment wired, you must first earn $100 (or equivalent currency).

Pseudonyms

How do I publish a book on KDP Select using a pseudonym?

When you set up your KDP account, use your real name and banking information (so you can get paid!). Then, when filling out the form to upload your ebook on KDP, simply type in your pen name rather than your real name under the contributors section.

How do I create an Author Central Page under my pseudonym? (You are allowed to manage up to three author pages under your one KDP account.)

1. Log into your regular Author Central page.
2. Click the "Books" tab at the top of the page.
3. Click the "Add more books" button.
4. A popup window appears asking for the book's title, author name (pseudonym), or ISBN of the pseudonym's book. Type in one of these items and click "Go."
5. A window appears showing one or more books. Under the correct title click "This is my book."
6. Yet another window pops up. Under the heading "Do you have a pen name?" click on

"Let us know." Now your Author Central page for your pseudonym has been created and your book has been added.

How do I log into my Author Central page with my pseudonym?

1. Log into Author Central under your real name account and password.
2. In the top right-hand corner of the page is a dropdown icon beside your name. Click that icon and all of your Author Central pages will appear, including those using your pseudonym.

What time do free promo days start?

All free promos begin at midnight Pacific Standard time and end at midnight Pacific Standard time on the date you selected. So you want to "book" your promo at least one day in advance.

What is "Author Rank"? Is it different from "Sales Rank"?

Amazon **Author Rank** (also called popularity) is based on sales of all your books relative to the sales of other authors on Amazon. You can check your Author Rank (using Author Central) for all ebooks, or you can check it in just your category. Currently, fiction author Melinda Leigh has the #1 Overall Author Rank.

Your **Sales Rank** (also called Best Seller Rank) is based on the number of books of each title you have sold on Amazon. This number appears in your book's Product Details page. For example, at the time of this book's publication, James Comey was ranked #1 in "Paid in Kindle Store" on Amazon.

Issues with epublishing

You may run into a few problems when using MS Word to upload your ebook to Amazon. Complex formatting like tables and graphics could cause conversion errors. Be sure to use the previewer on KDP if you think your ebook contains complex formatting. Don't expect the font sizes, margins, and page numbers that you set in Word to convert exactly in KDP. These settings will not apply because readers can adjust font sizes when using ereader devices.

NOTE: If you've copied and pasted numerous times from other documents and your manuscript is full of previous formatting, you can "nuke" your Word document to clear it up and make conversion easier. Simply copy and paste your manuscript into a plain text editor like Window's Notepad. Then copy and paste the document back to a new, blank Word document.

How do I check for plagiarism?

Want to see if someone, perhaps a co-writer, has plagiarized content from your website or blog that will be part of your book? Use Copyscape. Simply copy and paste the URL of your site into the field provided, and Copyscape will search the web for copies of your content. The service is free, or you can pay for more advanced features like daily web monitoring.

Here's the link: **http://www.copyscape.com/**

Do I need to register my book's copyright?

The short answer? No. The moment you create your book in a written format, it is automatically copyrighted. Here's the long answer from the United States Copyright Office

(**http://www.copyright.gov/**):
"Copyright protection subsists from the time the work is created in fixed form. The copyright in the work of authorship immediately becomes the property of the author who created the work. Only the author or those deriving their rights through the author can rightfully claim copyright."

For published works, the Copyright Office recommends you display your copyright in the following way:

The copyright symbol (@)
The year of first publication.
Your name.
For example: **@2011 John Doe**

What is NOT protected by copyright?

Here's a list (from the U.S. Copyright Office website) of what is NOT protected by federal copyright law:

- works that have not been fixed in a tangible form of expression (for example, choreographic works that have not been notated or recorded, or improvisational speeches or performances that have not been written or recorded)
- titles, names, short phrases, and slogans; familiar symbols or designs; mere variations of typographic ornamentation, lettering, or coloring; mere listings of ingredients or contents
- ideas, procedures, methods, systems, processes, concepts, principles, discoveries, or devices, as distinguished from a description, explanation, or illustration
- works consisting entirely of information that is common property and containing no original authorship (for example: standard calendars, height and weight charts, tape measures and rulers, and lists or tables taken from public documents or other common sources)

What if I just want to make a pdf of my book and sell it on my website?

You can totally do that! Selling your book directly from your website or blog means you receive most of the payment. Just remember that your payment processor will likely take a small percentage for each transaction.

Attaching a PayPal button to your website or blog is fairly easy. Here's a general overview:

1. Open a PayPal account and then upgrade it to a business account, which is free.
2. Go to "Merchandiser services" and follow the directions to "purchase" your PayPal button (it's free).
3. See if your website has a plug-in or widget that you can use to add the PayPal button more easily.
4. Add the button by copying and pasting the html script from PayPal onto your site. (If you're using some kind of text editor, make sure you select the "html" tab and paste the code there.)
5. Once you have added a PayPal (or other type of payment processor) button to your site, you will need to set up a page where customers can download your book immediately after they pay.

This article gives great in-depth detail about how to set up your PayPal button:
http://www.potpiegirl.com/how-to-sell-an-ebook-with-paypal

11 PRESS RELEASE TEMPLATE

Press releases come in many different formats, depending on whether you are using Associated Press style, a business format, or an academic style. But here is a general template that contains all the elements you need and should serve you well.

For examples of authors' press releases, go to http://service.prweb.com/who-uses-it/industry/authors-book-publishers/

There are free press release distribution sites that will post your press releases online and paid ones that will send them out to media outlets for you. Your best bet is to try a free service and also personally send out your press release to the editors of newspapers, magazines, and websites you want to feature your book. That way, you can write a nice, short introduction email or letter and target your specific, most important audiences.

Your name and contact info.
Email:
Phone:
Website:

FOR IMMEDIATE RELEASE

CATCHY HEADLINE IN BOLD AND ALL CAPS

CITY, STATE IN CAPS – Date – Begin with an attention-grabbing lead sentence and give the most important information in this first paragraph. What is your hook or angle? For example, you've just released a novel about zombies that explodes all the previous stereotypes of zombie-horror!

The next few paragraphs make up the body of press release. Give supporting information about the main idea (or hook) you raised in your first paragraph. Give quotations, etc... For example, describe in more detail your zombie book and give quotes from real people that reporters could interview for more information, such as book sellers who are surprised by its new approach.

Final paragraph: Relevant information about you (you once owned a zombie makeup studio) and your writing background. Mention your website and/or blog address.

###

To signify the end of your release, insert three hash marks.

Or, if your press release is two pages, write (more) in parenthesis at the bottom of the first page.

www.ingramcontent.com/pod-product-compliance
Lightning Source LLC
Chambersburg PA
CBHW071558270726
48657CB00026B/773